24 Common Mistakes Doctors Make That Destroy Their Business(es) And Retirement

Plus, Learn How To Quickly & Permanently Prevent or Solve Each Mistake

Jerry A. Jones
©2010 Jerry A. Jones
www.jerryjonesdirect.com

24 Common Mistakes Doctors Make That Destroy Their Busines(es) And Retirement

TABLE OF CONTENTS

1. Fail To Isolate and/or Mitigate Potential Risk 1

2. Put Off Creating a 2nd Income 3

3. Never Grasp What Makes a Business Successful 6

4. Improper Corporate Structure or No Corporate Structure 9

5. Accept Any or All Business Partners 11

6. Buy New Cars and Other Worthless, Depreciating Assets 13

7. Investing in Stocks and Not Knowing Why, or Worse, Knowing Why 16

8. Buying Unknowns 18

9. Over-Improve Things of Little Value 20

10. Purchase Second Homes 22

11. Listen To Conventional Wisdom 24

12. Shop in The Most Expensive Stores or Allow Family Members 26

13. Fail to Save Cash or Cash-Like Assets 28

14. Don't Believe Disasters Can Happen 31

15. Don't Take Regular, Scheduled Vacations 33

16. Buy vs Rent 36

17. Don't Understand or Monitor Practice Financials 38

18. Poor or Average Overall Financial Literacy 40

19. Get Involved in Scams - Tax Avoidance, Offshore Accounts, Etc. 42

20. Failure to File or Pay Taxes on Time 44

21. Keep Crap Not Needed 45

22. Pay Retail for any Item 47

23. Fail to Recognize Equity - Trademarks, Value in Systems, Etc. 50

24. Get Involved with a Non-Profit Board 53

25. **BONUS** Ignoring The Most Important Resource 55

Wrap-up 57

Resources 58

Copyright 2010
Jerry A. Jones
Published by Novus Venalicium, Inc.
All Rights Reserved.

Neither the author or publisher is an attorney or accountant. Neither is offering legal or accounting advice.

This is experiential information only and should not be relied on as a substitute for professional advice from licensed professionals in the accounting or legal arena.

Any reprinting, teaching, or otherwise disseminating any information included herein is a serious violation of copyright law and subject to hefty civil and criminal penalties which both author and publisher will aggressively pursue to protect their rights.

Neither the authors nor the publisher accept any liability whatsoever for any individual's actions or results in relying on the information in this publication. You're on your own and responsible for your own actions.

FOREWARD

No Dentist or businessman in America should have to face financial devastation. Aside from death or disability of a close family member or myself (I've been spared both thankfully), to say life was a struggle from mid-2008 thru the end of 2009, is an understatement; although, I certainly thank my lucky stars a personal financial collapse is <u>all</u> I had to deal with.

So many others are not as *lucky* in the *unlucky* department.

Although I'm not a Dentist myself, I've worked with hundreds and hundreds closely over the years and have studied their habits – both those ultra-successful and those not so much.

Here's what I've found: There's no reason to struggle. To be alone. To NOT know the secrets the wealthy have used for centuries to build wealth and live a life of <u>pleasant</u> leisure.

For that matter, there's just no reason why anyone should go through what I did.

Through education and enlightenment, it's all 100% avoidable. NO ONE has to take a difficult path. In fact, it's actually almost easier to avoid it than to make the mistakes.

Besides, there are no extra bonus points given on the Day of Reckoning for choosing the hard path. Nor should you be treated any differently for taking the smart path – the one others have paved before you after screwing-up themselves.

Through observation, I've found there are 3 types of Dentists and, in general, businessmen (or women):

1.) Those who've done 'it' wrong and eventually, using some kind of counsel or coaching, have taken corrective action. These are few and far between.

2.) Those that have done it wrong, continue to do so, but expect a new outcome, and;

3.) Those that have found the ugly path, worked to correct it, but keep adding and inventing new ways to screw up, hence never really making big headway.

The good news: there are some KEY fundamentals that I'll share with you, which I have uncovered the hard way, to AVOID being one of the **Dumb Doctors that Destroys Their Retirement or their Business(es)**.

Hang on, I'm not trying to insult you.

I can say all this because, I'm the third guy: I've screwed up, corrected it, tried to make smart choices in the interim, but continue to break new ground in the "moronic" moves department. In other words, it's been a challenge even for <u>me</u> to be *successful*.

Before I move on, can we agree on a definition of "successful?"

Here's mine: The point in life where family, friends and business balance in perfect harmony while providing a solid income and an even better, more stable and predictable <u>future</u> income.

I've reached this point, various times, for short periods. I've had millions. Lost millions. And I'm only 38.

Having more money *was* better at the time. Although, I found out, after losing it, what it was I was missing: family and friends.

So the challenge for me was getting it all put back together focusing on the right priorities for me: family first, friends second, business…third.

You see, I spent the last ten years like this: business first, family and friends third. No, there wasn't even a second. It was business.

It took making some major changes to "get it."

Anyway, I digress. It's always seemed as though as soon as one positive action occurs that can change the course, literally, of my business life for good and forever, one massive hiccup takes me out at the knees, and the struggle continues.

For example: I bought a business for pennies and sold it a decade later for a nice payday (my accountant couldn't believe it). Right after the sale, one of my businesses struggled with the loss of a key employee/provider/producer (a dentist), and I also was forced to sue a business partner for over $16,000,000 (any idea the kind of cash a lawsuit like that eats?) in another deal at the same time; all while the economy is the worst it's been since 1933; I'm staring at the possibility of financial ruin; and so on. In the interim, I started a new company whose primary clientele are women under the age of 25. Ugh. Just make it easy and feed me some poison.

The last 24 months have been real eye-opening for me. I've weathered a major financial hardship, which will likely take a decade of hard work to completely clean up, I've wrote checks to the IRS and state governments well into the six figures, I've struggled to keep my immediate and extended family together, and I could go on.

Now, you might be asking why I would even consider writing this tome about screwing up. It's a valid question. After all, this wasn't something I threw together without a lot of forethought and planning. I had to ask and answer a lot of hard questions of myself.

But, ultimately, why I decided to write this book, is twofold:

First, there's the Karma thing. I'm a big believer in what you sow, so shall you shall reap.

Last, it all boils down to me wanting to help current and past clients and other dentists think through some very damaging actions and possibly correct them or even better, prevent them before they occur. The profession has been good to me and I just can't think, at least right now, of a better way to give back.

Costly mistakes have been a specialty of mine and many of my clients over the years. If you can learn from others, it's a big short-cut. To a happy life. To a financially successful, low-stress life.

Let's get started. And hey, thanks for reading.

1

Fail To Isolate and/or Mitigate Potential Risk

There's a reason this common mistake is #1. It's obvious to me at this point – I've seen more people ruined by failing to isolate risk, so much so, that it'd be a challenge to find one business person close to me that has at some point, not lost a lot or it *all* from not <u>segmenting</u> or <u>compartmentalizing</u> their risk.

I'll give you a few areas where you should get legal and tax advice to minimize risk and also, more importantly, or as importantly, avoid becoming a target of predators and creditors.

First, separate your assets and own as many things as possible in your 401(k) or IRA. Both savings and retirement vehicles are, unless fraud is proven, shielded from creditors and predators – they also survive the ultimate, yet temporary ruin of bankruptcy – in other words, you get to keep them.

If you have a dental practice, there's no reason why a separate company you *control* shouldn't own the dental equipment – you know, the big stuff – the chairs, computer systems, building – everything except the consumable sundries.

I'll dig a little further. My dental practice management business is segmented into two areas: the management side and the equipment side. The management side which has employees, and buys dental supplies like the consumables, is an S Corp. The other side, the one that leases the space and the equipment to the doctor, is an LLC. So the business has no value – one without the other.

I also owned, prior-to my bankruptcy, several apartment units: a six-plex, several duplexes and a couple of small office buildings. All but the six-plex are in separate entities. Each duplex has its own LLC. I kept them separate so that in the event one property has a legal problem none of the others are involved or affected.

A step further – My wife and I have separate bank accounts. She's on the mortgage and the deed of the house, I'm on neither.

Another strategy to protect your home: do not own it outright. If you have little or no equity in your home, it's not a target for the IRS or a creditor. It has no value if they can't sell it quickly for surplus cash.

Lastly, and this is critical: if you serve on a board of directors, which I cover in another section of this book, be sure you have adequate protection. More on that later.

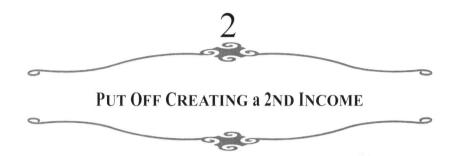

PUT OFF CREATING a 2ND INCOME

Dentists and other medical providers are at the greatest risk for losing it all if they should suffer an injury preventing them from practicing. You've heard the story of the dentist – broken hand, leg, neck, paralyzed, stroke, heart attack whatever.

All of a sudden, a practice that produced $200,000 a year in net profit is now producing zero and the doc is relying on supplemental disability income to make house payments, tuition payments, retirement funding and all the other bills we <u>all</u> seem to rack up. It's stressful.

It's ugly. Guy has to go back to work.

Now, to avoid ALL this crap, the smart doctor is going to realize from Day 1, that he's not invincible, and completely vulnerable to accidents and financial disasters.

What's saved me more than once, is my inability to focus

on just one project at a time. I seem to do better the more ball juggling I do. After selling my core business to an employee a few years ago, I decided I'd better ramp up another business that was doing nothing at the time, but draining me emotionally and financially: my dental practice management business.

I knew I had Fridays and Saturdays available in the office and it wasn't being used for anything. I'd heard about and talked to a few dental assisting school owners and decided after doing some basic market research, I could add one and build-up an additional revenue stream.

That was 2007. It's been over three years since I took the plunge and started the process to get the school up and going. Today, it's an operating private, state-licensed school educating young men and women about dental assisting, and soon, front office management. I also learned that a local community college is dropping their medical office assisting program, so there's a good chance we'll be adding other, adjunct opportunities for our students.

This second business, along with the dental practice management company were responsible for saving my bacon. If not for them, I'm not quite sure what would have happened. After financial disaster struck, the best thing going for me was more than one business opportunity I could ramp up.

I highly encourage every dentist I meet and get to know to create or buy a second business of some kind they either own and operate or just control. I can see a dental assisting school being a great business to own with an IRA, especially since most dentists I know don't actually *work* in the school – they merely staff it and control the operations.

Still other dentists I know have started "info" businesses where they have created a nice sideline income that often exceeds or matches their practice income.

Former client, Charley Martin, DDS, is a good example. Chris Bowman, DDS, is another example. Both have created nice little businesses that can operate out of their spare office at home and create a nice income. Many other dentists have added different aspects of real estate investing to their businesses – like buying rental properties that someone else manages and buying my favorite, tax liens or tax deeds.

What's your passion outside of dentistry? Monetize it and you, too, can sleep worry-free at night, just in case an accident does happen.

3

NEVER GRASP WHAT MAKES A BUSINESS SUCCESSFUL

I got lucky. Early-on in my business career, I was mentored by some real sharp tacks. They knew what made a business successful: **smart marketing, recurring, ongoing revenue and low expenses.**

To create that recurring revenue – an annuity if you will – takes specific abilities, namely marketing and selling.

If you know how to write copy (copywriting), or ads, or <u>understand the power of emotional direct response advertising</u>, you can make a fortune just by putting words on paper.

I've made millions for my companies because I learned how to write ads that sold; and to make sure I had capable, qualified people on the other end that could CLOSE the sale I was able to "set up" from my marketing.

And the best part of this skill is it is portable and can be used anywhere on ANY company. Once you grasp the basics, it's amazing what you can do with a few carefully crafted sentences.

As soon as people learn you can drive business with your marketing, hang on; the demand will start and soon you will be getting requests to help other business owners with their marketing. I got a request one Easter Sunday, from someone I went to college with to help them coordinate their marketing with the opening of a new winery.

Just this past week, I made a decision that was pretty pivotal I believe: I dropped a weekly commitment I had made with a group of people so I could focus more on the advertising and marketing of the dental assisting school and the dental practice.

I realized I was holding my own income and that of key team members back because I have not been putting 100% of my efforts into those two businesses. *So that's changing.*

Those two opportunities will now become the focal point of my week vs. being on the back burner and less of a priority.

One lesson I learned early was: wherever the money is coming from, GO THERE and re-double your efforts.

Well, money's coming from the dental office and the school. Why am I worried about anything OTHER than those two places?

It's an obvious question, but, sometimes the obvious can take us down, too. Simplify the questions you ask yourself, like, "Where is the money coming from? How can I double it, triple it? Then, how can I replace myself?"

There's no challenge these days in becoming overwhelmed. It seems to go with the territory of being in business, you know?

4

IMPROPER CORPORATE STRUCTURE OR NO CORPORATE STRUCTURE

In Chapter 1, regarding the "mitigating or segmenting risk" mistake, I see a lot of business owners, dentists, too, with improper corporate or no corporate structuring. Not only is their tax bill higher than it should be, they are also exposing themselves to unnecessary risk. In business, a good attorney and CPA and tax planner do not COST you one red cent. They MAKE you money and keep you out of trouble.

This may sound unbelievable, but I can assure you it's true: If I had invested just $1200 into an attorney to have him create a limited liability operating agreement vs. just reviewing it myself and doing a quick "self-approval" on it, I could potentially have been spared a major amount of trouble on more than one occasion.

You see, I entered into an equal 25% partnership with three others. Because of the way the LLC operating agreement was written and structured, some really stupid things could legally happen. It cost me millions. But you know, I had the chance. I had other "smart" people tell me their horror stories and I didn't listen. My WIFE even told me what I should do.

But, I'm male. I'm smarter than everyone else so I had to learn it first-hand. Let me tell you, it sucked. And, it added 10 years onto my retirement.

5

ACCEPT ANY OR ALL BUSINESS PARTNERS

There are very, very, very, very few circumstances when you should consider having a business partner. Please don't take this section lightly and think there are exceptions. I've had all sorts of wild things happen and perhaps you have, too.

These are the conditions that must be met if I have business partners (all of these conditions <u>must</u> be met):

a) I'm the majority owner and controlling interest – they are silent and NOT deadly.
b) I trusted them with my life once and they are still alive.
c) Ethics, morals, needs and wants are in alignment with mine.
d) No spouses are involved.
e) MY attorney writes the corporate agreement and has given me every advantage possible.
f) If they don't put money in, they lose their interest proportionately. NO FREE rides.

g) All the money's committed upfront and no future expenses are expected.

h) None of the partners NEEDS the money in the partnership to live on or retire on.

If you violate these rules, you will regret it. It's only from taking a few hits I know this and now stick by it as Gospel truth!

6

Buy New Cars And Other Worthless, Depreciating Assets

The dumbest money you can spend is on a new vehicle of almost ANY kind.

I'm going to assume you know why, but will tell you anyway: Depreciation. The second you drive off the car lot, just TRY to get back what you paid for it!

I bought a 2008 Toyota Highlander Hybrid. Paid $43,000 for it. One year later, it sold at auction for $23,000. In one year, it "lost" $20,000 in value.

One other car example. Late 2008, I voluntarily turned over another vehicle – a G-500 Mercedes. Same situation: this car on any car lot: $45,000 to $50,000, USED. It sold at auction for $31,000. New, it was over $90,000.

If you don't know the auction or wholesale value, how can you really know the true value of anything?

Unless from day one you expect it to be a collector's item, new cars are a fast way to "no or negative-equity hell!"

In a period of 8 years, I bought or leased over 8 vehicles. I spent close to $400,000 on fancy ego-boosting cars. Dumbest thing I ever did.

I was so enthralled with myself that I actually bought two cars, very similar to each other (a Mercedes G-500 and a G-55) – one for me and one for my wife.

These cars alone were close to $160,000 (and that doesn't include any of the interest I paid, either!). WHAT THE HECK? (See above and the value of one of these at auction!)

Who in their *right* mind needs two $80,000 cars? Not me or my wife. I can tell you that. I look just as sexy in my 1987 Toyota Camry as I did that fancy Mercedes G-55!

Look, I love new cars. I love fast, expensive cars. But, how can anyone justify spending $3100 a month in car payments and another $450 a month on top of that for car insurance?! Do you realize I could have paid for one of my kids' college with what I spent on those?!

Listen: <u>buy used cars</u> – two to three years old, with warranty remaining on them. Buy reliable cars like a Honda or Toyota. Most of them, if not all, are now at least put together here in the US, so you're certainly keeping US citizens employed.

Just whatever you do, do not buy new. Let some other egotistical moron take the depreciation hit.

Rather than investing your hard-earned money into assets that immediately lose value, invest your money into adjunct/related businesses, safe-harbors (like Tax Liens or Tax Deeds) or YOURSELF.

When the s*** hits the fan, there are a few things that survive the worst financial disasters: skills and businesses you control but don't personally, legally own, are the two main things.

Don't take this for granted.

7

INVESTING IN STOCKS AND NOT KNOWING WHY, OR WORSE, KNOWING WHY!

Stock picking is NOT a past-time. It's NOT a sport. It's a serious game that not even brokers with decades of experience have figured out. Otherwise, there'd be more stock picking millionaires, several in my family to boot. (And those are not dim-witted souls I might add!)

Now, keep in mind here, I'm not an expert. What I do know about stocks though is they are sketchy, have no relationship to the actual business they are sold by and it's actual profit/loss performance.

In other words, a business can be doing well, but if it's in a "sector" that is doing poorly, say, it's an energy sector stock, or healthcare sector stock, then the stock price can drop, even with rising profits in the business.

A stock and the business it is sold from, are two completely different animals.

Picking stocks, plain and simple, <u>is</u> gambling.

If you don't understand what you are doing and are buying stocks because someone said it's a "sure thing" you can expect to lose your money to some smarter fella selling the company stocks "short."

And, if you don't know what that means, you're surely doing the wrong thing.

I'm a big believer in tax liens. Each month, I buy several hundred dollars worth of Arizona tax liens. I earn 16% interest, and, it's guaranteed by the government.

8

BUYING UNKNOWNS

If you really don't know WHAT you are buying, why are you buying it?

I'll take the "average" dentist, whatever that means, as example. Let's say the "average" dentist, kind of like the average Joe, is at a trade show. A dental trade show. Maybe it's the state or regional show and there's a few thousand people rummaging around. Some trying to learn, but most trying to sell.

The vendors at a dental trade show of state dental association meeting are numerous. There's the laser guys, the advertising guys, the instrument guys, the financial (let us separate your money from you) guys, the handpiece guys, the latest-fricking-hot-air-gas-compressed-laser-light-gizmo guys, and so on. You know what I'm talking about.

They all have their product or service tied to a specific ROI they've somehow conjured up. So, "if you buy MY widget, it'll provide you a 10:1 return in just days." "Or, if you buy MY gizmo, you'll never have to do X again."

Lots of promises, right?

You know what I mean don't you?

Well, unless you KNOW for certain, and know someone that has DONE IT, or bought it, you oughta hang tight. There's no glory most of the time, if you're conservative, like I now am, in being a pioneer. They seem to get their arses full of arrows, and that my friend, is painful.

9

OVER-IMPROVE THINGS OF LITTLE VALUE

Ever watch the do-it-yourself shows or home improvement shows on cable? You know, the HGTV shows where some moron takes a mobile home and puts $25,000 into it thinking he'll get $26,000 back (Not a chance bubba. It's a mobile home!).

What I am talking about here is similar. If you buy an old POS (piece of s _ _ _), make sure it has some value once restored – or, make sure when you BUY, that you're buying *far* below even the potential wholesale value. Truthfully, there are a lot of things you should not restore – the economics just don't make sense.

On the other hand, some of the best quick money you can spend to have a fast impact in your office is on décor. If you can invest a few thousand a year in décor, it comes back several fold – people actually want to hang around nice things – so getting rid of the shag carpet and old vinyl torn-up and duct-taped chairs is one place where you might have a hard time overspending.

Just be careful. Ask yourself: If I invest X, am I going to get X back and then some? If you don't know, beware and go find someone that can help you.

10

Purchase 2nd Homes

I was going to be ginger on approaching this. But, let me just say this: Second homes are STUPID. Yes, DUMB. If you own a second home, this is one of the most ridiculous things you could possibly fall into.

I've owned a few homes in my time. By far and away, my 2nd home purchase in a vacation destination area, which was initially done for a quick fix and flip, was one of the dumbest things imaginable, that I've consciously done.

Renting a home anywhere you want to be for any length of time is a far better use of your funds than owning. I don't even care if you plan on retiring somewhere. (As of this writing. Some day, the economics may change!)

Do the math. Compare current rental rates for a similar home where you want to retire or buy a second home, with what it will cost you to OWN that same home.

The insurance, HOA fees (if any), utilities, property taxes, mortgage payment, lost opportunity on your cash will eat you alive. (I've yet to see a housing market in a resort area that maintains its values through a recession – there might be one someplace, but it's not anywhere I want to be, and besides, it's likely still cheaper to RENT in that very same area!) will eat you alive.

Couple all those factors with the hassles of home ownership like maintenance, maybe putting it in a rental pool (Trust me: stupid idea – even the high-end homes like the one I had in Sunriver, Oregon get thrashed, and usually it was the "higher-end, wealthy" renters that destroyed things regularly), dealing with a property management firm, not being close by to use it as often as you'd like, and so on, WHY would you want to own?

I'll tell you: it's all about your ego. There isn't a good reason you can give me that makes economic sense unless you have no kids and you'd spend at least ¾ or more of your time there. It was a hard realization for me to come to, but I did. It's about the ego. Period.

11

LISTEN TO CONVENTIONAL WISDOM

CW is conventional wisdom. Just about every thought you have has some CW associated with it. In other words, someone, somewhere, has decided that there's a standard answer to just about every question.

Everything from running your dental business to hiring/firing employees, saving for retirement, how many hours you should work each day and so on. There are standards out there and most people that stick with the standard CW gets what everyone else gets.

For instance: CW says businesses should be open 5 to 7 days each week. I know people that have limited their hours to 3 or 4 days per week and have increased their incomes doing it.

I know a lot of business owners that don't employ full-time receptionists to answer their phones; instead, they have certain hours when phones are answered live. My office is the same way.

Still others have adopted a "Straight-6" approach to scheduling dental pts. That simply means pts are seen for a six-hour straight period vs. a split 4-hour and 4-hour schedule like CW might suggest. In fact, my office operates that way on Fridays. In 2011, we'll be moving to a more productive schedule. If your office doesn't operate in the most productive manner possible, are you overworking yourself and your team for less money? I'd wager a bet on it.

You see, people that follow CW get what the herd-following CW gets: average incomes and average results.

Mavericks go against the grain; always have since the dawn of time. If you're a maverick, sure you'll face challenges, but the potential rewards are amazing. It also leads to a much more rewarding life than being so boring and just going along with CW. Ugh.

Contrarians make buckets of money. It pays, many times, to do the opposite of what your fellow dentist is doing, especially if that guy's following the herd. Be different. It's a great way to position yourself in a crowded market and really stand out and make a name for yourself.

If you look at history, pioneers got the arrows, the notoriety and most of the time, the glory they deserved.

If you want to be a regular Joe, that's OK, but, don't complain about having a boring life or being an average income earner!

12

SHOP IN THE MOST EXPENSIVE STORES OR ALLOW FAMILY MEMBERS TO

I'm really fortunate. Although my wife loves Nordstroms®, she never has been the kind of person to black out a credit card on a shopping trip or been overloaded with bags and unable to get to her car when she's on her way home.

She's a bargain shopper. She likes Wal-Mart®, as do I, and will hold out for a bargain. She's conservative with her money and mine, too. She values a good deal and doesn't take anything we have or have worked hard for, for granted. Every dollar counts to her and it means a lot to me and sets a great example for our two girls.

If you've got a spouse that is out-of-control or can't place a value on the hard work you're putting in, you'd better fix that problem now before it gets worse.

I've got one friend whose wife will easily drop $3000 to $5000 on a trip to Nordies. He hates it, but he puts up with it.

Me, I'd fire her. Done. Finito. Through. Adios, Amiga.

And, he's killing himself from stress and work, trying to keep his business alive, and she keeps spending. Her closet IS a store – no joke. Her friends come over to get clothes from her all the time.

Look…it's clothes. Clothes are clothes. I like nice ones, but I sure as heck don't need a pair of jeans that cost more an hour of my billable time. I mean, $500 for a pair of jeans?! I'm just as happy in a $17 pair of Wal-Mart® khakis!

I'll let those folks who're mightier than I with the checkbook buy those high-priced items.

13

FAIL TO SAVE CASH OR CASH-LIKE ASSETS

Cash and cash equivalents are <u>unrivaled</u> when it comes to solving problems (In some economic times, these equivalents are <u>even</u> <u>more</u> critical).

In our current economic mess, which seems to repeat itself about every 20 years, which would indicate the publics' memory lasts about 10 years, or half that time, the biggest tool or biggest hammer to get anything done or to make hordes of money is CASH or its equivalents.

What are cash equivalents? This, compliments of wikipedia.org:

> "Cash and cash equivalents are the most liquid assets found within the asset portion of a company's balance sheet. Cash equivalents are assets that are readily convertible into cash, such as money market holdings, short-term government bonds or Treasury bills, marketable securities and commer-

cial paper.

"Cash equivalents are distinguished from other investments through their short-term existence; they mature within 3 months whereas short-term investments are 12 months or less, and long-term investments are any investments that mature in excess of 12 months. Another important condition a cash equivalent needs to satisfy is that the investment should have insignificant risk of change in value. Example: an investment in shares cannot be considered a cash equivalent, but preference shares acquired shortly before their specified redemption date can be."

I like GOLD. Yes, GOLD. In fact, I think everyone ought to have a certain percentage, depending on their age until retirement, in gold. Not paper that says you own gold, but the hard asset itself. Preferably Loonies (Canadian Gold Coins) or Eagles (American Gold Eagles are sort of the Gold Standard if you will).

There are places where you can buy physical gold. Do a search online for the city you live in or the nearest city of 50,000 or more and Gold and you'll find what you're looking for. There are online retailers as well. Be wary. Some are frauds.

Something to keep in mind: The price of gold fluctuates. It's a commodity. Like any publicly traded commodity in a worldwide market, you have to know WHEN to buy gold. It doesn't, in my opinion, always make sense to buy gold. NO commodity has ever always increased in value.

As economic situations change in the US and worldwide, the price of gold will come back down. As I write this, it's about $900 an ounce. In the last 10 years, I've paid *under* $300 an ounce. It WILL go back down.

However, that doesn't mean you shouldn't convert some of your assets to gold especially if you are a doom and gloomer.

If you buy gold all the time, at all prices, you'll end up averaging out your investment so you can usually then convert to cash or use gold to buy something anytime and get a reasonable deal. (Dollar Cost Averaging so to speak.) I'm not an expert in this area – I just know enough to be dangerous to myself and others.

The point to all this is make darn sure you have assets that can be converted to the currency of the day and done so easily.

If you honestly think life in the good ol' US is always going to be rosy, you have a rude awakening just waiting for you.

14

Don't Believe Disasters Can Happen

If you don't think disasters can happen here and to you, may I remind you of 9/11?

We've been very lucky the last 50 or 60 years.

That was as close as we've come to a major systemic meltdown ever. And, right here on our soil. We were attacked by radical nutcases.

It can and odds are, will happen again. When it does, DO YOU have a plan in place for you and your family to react and actually survive?

Yeah, this sounds gloomy, but hey, it's the reality of the 21st century and to think otherwise means you'll be one not making it through the chaos and onto the next chapter.

Here in my house, which is 7 miles from town, we have

generators (2 – one was given to me), stored water, food for 4 for at least 30 days (bought at Costco® for a few hundred bucks and it's in a 5-gallon bucket and good for like 10 years), lots of canned food always, and yes, I even have several different means of self-defense, too.

Am I worried? Do I live in fear?

No.

I'm *prepared*. And, if something does happen, it's my job to protect my family and that's what I'll do. YOU should do the same. Be smart. Don't let a disaster strike and make you look like a fool or less of a man.

Shoot, just pretend you live in the outback and you HAVE to have rations in case some weird natural disaster were to happen. And if you do live in the pucker brush, you probably are already prepared and just don't think too much of it. At this point, I don't either. I just feel better knowing I can do what it will take.

15

Don't Take Regular, Scheduled Vacations

This might sound out of place in a book like this.

I've learned the fastest way to burn-out for the average human is to not take regular, scheduled breaks from work…and sometimes, from family.

All that working too much leads to is an imbalanced, completely out-of-whack life and worse, distorted *reality*.

How do I know?

I worked for about six straight years until I realized I didn't have a relationship with my wife or my daughter. Sure, I had money. More than I could spend. I had it "all."

Except, I didn't have what mattered most: my family in my life.

Today, in fact, for the last two plus years, I have put my family first. All else, and I don't care what it is, is second.

Friends, work, businesses, outside relationships. It's all secondary. <u>IT HAS TO BE</u>.

I don't need to tell you that when you die, all you got is the cold bedsheet over you, a hard, uncomfortable and unforgiving bed beneath and a few close family members and if you're lucky, *real lucky*, a few close friends who really give a damn and appreciate you for who you are/were.

Today, I fit business in around my family. When the kids are in bed, I write. A lot. In fact, 1AM or midnight at the earliest, is my bedtime and oddly, it's the best hours for me. I write well, am alert and enjoy the silence of the evening.

YOU should, too. Perhaps your hours are not like mine. Doesn't matter. When you're working, your kids are maybe in school. Work hard. When they are out, give them all you got. Same goes for your spouse. Treat him or her with the love, respect and honor you SAID you would if/when you tied the knot.

If you have cancerous people (those with bad attitudes, etc.) in your life, eradicate 'em and move on. It's the most amazing feeling in the world when you move out of a bad relationship. It'll be replaced with a better relationship almost immediately. I love how the universe handles things like that.

Anyway – back to vacations and mini vacations. Take them. Take 3 and 4 day weekends regularly. And I mean, at least a few times a month.

If you MUST work 5 or 6 days a week, you've got your priorities all screwed up and something, like it or not, will give. That's not what you want. You want to make the choices before someone else or something else makes them for you. Stay in control. Defense sucks, so always be playing and planning offensively in every aspect of your life – business and personal. Got it?

I take long weekends at least 2 times a month. My wife and kids love it. I'm more energized and more useful to everyone around AND I get a lot more done when I know I have an agenda of vacations to follow vs. an agenda at work!

16

Buy vs. Rent

Most things you believe you'll need long-term (10 years and longer is long-term; at least my thinking right now), buy if you can. If it's short-term, lease.

There are exceptions of course. When it comes to autos, you really need to do two things: talk to your CPA and get his/her input *after* you take a long, hard look at your buying & driving habits.

If you do high miles, buying probably best. If you are a low miles car driver, own your own business, have good credit, really think hard about the leasing route.

Now, when it comes to office items, if it's a high-production gizmo, think: lease. Specifically, copiers. The technology changes so quickly and the efficiencies do as well, that if you buy, you probably couldn't afford to own it for more than 4 to 5 years if you use it daily with high print runs.

I do suggest if you are making a major buying decision and it's a choice between a purchase and a lease, a quick call to your CPA can potentially save you big money. Know this: the person selling you the "thing" just wants to get paid and they'll pretty much tell you what you want to hear as long as they get the sale. So be careful and don't be afraid to spend a few dollars on researching what's best for your particular situation.

17
Don't Understand Or Monitor Practice Financials

This section starts with a question: How often do you review practice financials? Specifically, your P&L and Balance Sheet? Also, do you know the difference between accrual and cash basis accounting and how it applies specifically to your businesses?

Look, if you don't have a season-by-season, month-to-month handle on your books, you're not really on top of how your business is doing.

If you wait until end-of-month reports from your CPA or quarterly reports from your CPA to tell you how you are doing, you're crazy. Off the mark. Setting yourself up for a huge disappointment or worse, failure.

I spent the first three years in business learning the cycles and then advertising/marketing against the down cycles to bring some sort of stability to my business. I spent the last 3 years watching what happens with dental practices with my own office, SofTouch™ Family Dental Group, Inc. I've learned when the ugly times are and what to do in advance, to counter-act the downturns that come every year at the same times.

If you are tracking your income and expenses in an accounting program like Quickbooks®, then you can literally graph out the months when income's down or months when expenses are unusually high.

There are other methods to this that integrate with this thinking and help prepare monthly expense budgets for you.

In other words, if you have months when expenses are high, say when Dexis® and Dentrix® support payments are due and you know the stroke on those is going to be a few thousand bucks, if you save monthly for this, you can amortize the expense out; and you should do that with all annual expenses so the "hit" on your pocket book is spread out even though you may only pay that bill once a year.

These are the kinds of things that studying your "books" teaches you. The better you know your income/expense reports and what your balance sheet looks like (or should look like and you've got a map to get you there), the better you'll do in your overall quest for financial independence.

18

Poor Or Average Overall Financial Literacy

First of all, if you're reading this book, you're above average in your pursuit of knowledge that can get you to the next level. And, I congratulate you for that.

However, if I failed to bring this point home, I'd be doing many a disservice.

I know some business owners that don't understand the basics of cash flow models, of finance in business, or, even how to balance a checkbook.

I also know many that buy things first before checking to see if they had money in the bank to keep the transaction from going south.

I'm very familiar with still more that if you asked them what their percentage of overhead was in relationship to their practice's income, they'd have no clue. Or, what it cost them in time and money to gain a new client. Lose a client. Reactivate a client (read: patients).

There are guys and gals out there that don't even understand why it makes sense financially to have high debt on your primary residence. An advanced answer, after the pat answer of, "because it's the last single tax write-off you can get without owning a business," would be, "It's actually an asset protection & lawsuit prevention strategy."

On the flip side, it's wonderful having no debt whatsoever on a property so that your only responsibility is upkeep, taxes and insurance.

But you see, there's a cost to that freedom. Isn't that the way it always is? For every action…there's an equal and…

Yep. That's the way it goes. You have to decide, at different points in your life, what is to your advantage. Based on my age, my ugly past financial experience, I can honestly say, high debt on our primary house was a blessing.

Get educated on basic financial literacy. Read, <u>Rich Dad, Poor Dad</u>. Get Robert Kiyosaki's game, Cash Flow®. It's a great game and will let you know, who, in your family, is on target for overall life success.

A few things that financially illiterate people do:

    a. Don't invest in income-producing properties
    b. Buy wasting assets (Chapter 16)
    c. Invest in stocks (or company stock that is offered to them) they don't understand. Instead of choosing "YOU, Inc."

19

GET INVOLVED IN SCAMS - TAX AVOIDANCE, OFFSHORE ACCOUNTS, ETC.

Why do so many people fall for the "too good to be true and really are" scams? I've heard of more dentists loosing their butts from tax schemes than you can imagine.

The effort it takes to avoid taxes could be better spent making more money to pay taxes. If you owe 'em, pay 'em. And, don't put it off.

Interest and penalties charged by the IRS and state governments are very, very high. One year, I had to re-direct my tax funds and use them elsewhere. It was, in hindsight a bad idea. It cost me well over $20,000 in penalties and interest. NOT a bright idea. And, I certainly didn't get $20,000 in benefit for the re-direct, either.

The tax man's heard about every story possible and they've seen virtually ever iteration of tax avoidance. Their job is about collecting taxes. They know where people try to hide income.

Bottom line: tax shelters don't exist. Offshore accounts, unless for legit purposes, which I have no idea what that might even be, aren't necessary and attract attention. Use your head, pay your taxes and realize, if it sounds *that* good, it probably deserves extra careful scrutiny.

20

FAILURE TO FILE OR PAY TAXES ON TIME

The worst "bank" you could ever want to owe is the IRS. When you earn income, pay the taxes. Don't keep the tax money from the feds or state government. The expense associated with not paying on time is very high and is that way for a reason: to deter people from paying late.

File on time or file an extension. Pay your taxes on the 15th or by the 15th of October, same year, to keep yourself out of hot water and paying HUGE fees…that are NOT tax deductible!

What else could I possibly say on this? Nothing. It's a pretty simple issue.

21

Keep Crap Not Needed

Ever spring clean? It's one of the best things to do on a day when not much else is happening. De-cluttering is a great way to get your "area" cleared as well as your mind. A desk littered with piles is OK and for some, they're *Modus Operandi*. I happen to be one that works that way. As long as it's not bugging me when I'm working, it's good where it's at.

There are a few places you should keep de-cluttered: your hard drive on your computer is one.

Another, for sure, is an office where the public interacts with you.

You've heard about the CEO that has two offices. One's for show and one's for actual work.

The "show" version is clean, de-cluttered, simple. The "getting-it-done" desk is a disaster.

However, high-clutter is common among entrepreneurs (or, people like me keep writing it so it has become accepted and so businesspeople just say, "Screw it! Everyone's like this!").

eBay® is a great place to get rid of unwanted items. Especially old or no-longer-in-use dental equipment. I have a few items I need to auction myself in fact! Craigslist.org also works well. In fact, we use Craigslist.org for finding new employees. It works much better for us than monster.com and other paid sites.

PAY RETAIL FOR ANY ITEM

I'm convinced most of the world pays way too much for everything they buy. Sometimes though, I believe that's what makes the world go round. However, doesn't mean *you* have to join the ranks in spending more money than you should!

Here's a perfect example: One Saturday morning I was dropping one of my daughter's friends off at her house. I know the parents really well and have for several years. The girl's dad and I were talking about landscaping. It was spring, so that was on a lot of people's minds right then here in Oregon.

We quickly narrowed it down to how much he was paying a gardener vs. what I was paying. We have similar landscapes. He was paying $180 a month and I was paying $265.

Granted, my guys are bonded and insured and I'm thinking his are not (what I used to refer to when I was landscaping many years ago as "scalpers" – if these guys get hurt on your property, if they are not bonded and insured, they could sue you!). I'm also wondering if he's going to fertilize or if they will for him? And, are they going to charge him extra when they do? Gee, I sound like Andy Rooney.

Then there are cars. Houses. Boats. Vacations. Dental supplies. Rent. Insurance.

Businesses, even yours and mine, are designed to provide something of value in return for cash. You should be carefully scrutinizing expenses with your spouse, your office management team and even on your own guilty pleasures…That extra cup of fancy flavored coffee, etc. – you know what I'm talking about.

If you're overpaying, just think: you're overworking *to overpay someone else that doesn't benefit you but robs you of time you could be spending with your family or relaxing and enjoying the fruits of your labors!*

When I found out my friend was paying $80 a month less than me, it annoyed me. It also motivated me to check pricing with other companies that could do a similar job with similar end-results.

However, I've had other companies bid and I know from that experience, the company I was paying $265 a month to was reputable, safe, good, and they listened to what we wanted done and balanced that with what can and should be done.

When it comes to supplies, if your Henry Schein guy or your Burkhart guy isn't discounting your orders, he should be.

We buy 99% of our supplies through Schein. I can tell you our rep is peeling the prices back a long way compared to sticker in the catalog – big time. He knows our business, too, and has good suggestions for us when he picks up something interesting at other offices – so he's good at doing the "added-value thing."

23

Fail To Recognize Equity - Trademarks, Value In Systems, Etc.

Recently, I filled out a 1-page form, and submitted an application to the Oregon Secretary of State's office to file a trade mark on the name SofTouch™ as in SofTouch™ Family Dental.

Doing that one simple action increased the value of my management company a few points. The cost? $50.

I started using the name to promote practices in September 2003. That information was on the application as was the use of the "mark," meaning, etc.

I did this one other time and I believe it really paid off. I had a coaching group for my clients, which at the time, were all dentists, called, Personal Dental Coach™. Now, that mark and coaching business are owned by Erickson Marketing Communications, Inc. One of the things their attorney really liked was the fact I'd trademarked one of my business names and processes.

Cool. It was easy. Cost me $50. I sold that business for a nice profit, too.

Then there's systems. McDonalds®, is a system to find a sweet piece of real estate on a busy corner or road, open a restaurant that sells cheeseburgers and make those cheeseburgers and restaurants taste and look the same all over the world.

Roy Kroc invented a system to do that. His system is worth BILLIONS of dollars. They've served BILLIONS of customers (me included).

Ask yourself this: would you pay a little extra or even a lot extra for a dental practice that was all set-up and systemized with every aspect you could imagine, and to the nth degree, or would you settle for a half-wit practice, no systems, just some equipment and partially-trained employees and no procedures in writing on how to collect money, bill for services, deal with patients, etc., etc.?

I'll take the systemized business.

In fact, I bought then later sold a newsletter business "system" come to think of it. I bought it from a dentist, changed/improved on the product/service/ systems, and then, 10 years later, sold it for a HUGE multiple of what I originally paid. What a deal!

What I learned recently from an asset planning attorney was that I can place the ownership of any trademark or systems I've developed into a family limited partnership (FLIP) and with some magic I guess, lease it to the business. Big corporations use this kind of thing all the time. They will "sell" their intellectual property (IP) to an entity that most likely is related, then lease the right to use the "mark" – whether a trademark or service mark, and pay the entity a royalty for the use. Imagine if your IRA owned the entity which all the trademarks and service marks or systems you set up were "inside"…TAX FREE revenue to your IRA is what I see.

24

GET INVOLVED WITH A NON-PROFIT BOARD

Would you believe it if I told you, I also had to learn the hard way about non-profits and serving on their boards of directors?

This all happened in 2008, too. (I was besieged with fun, eh?)

So along about July 2008, I was notified of an emergency board meeting. I went. It merely added to the drama I was already engulfed with at the beach on the large condo/marina project going up in smoke and other related messes.

I found out the director/founder and his wife had given themselves unauthorized pay raises, used corporate funds to adopt a child, gone on "junkets" and purchased over $3 million in property at inflated rates giving the former owners some kind of tax break for a donation. Anyway, it was ugly.

Today, the case is pending before the Oregon Department of Justice and I don't believe it's over. The number of people affected by this guy and gal are huge – clients of the company suffered, donors were bilked and volunteers like myself and the other board members have been hung out to dry not just with having to unwind all this, but a massive amount of potential liability.

It all goes back to one time, at some meeting, I heard some speaker say, "Never get involved as a board member unless…" and he named off a bunch of conditions and I'm sure if I were listening, this entity would have fit the test for NOT volunteering for.

But again, I'm a male. I don't listen too well sometimes, and know more than everyone else. Sound familiar?

25

BONUS IGNORE THE MOST IMPORTANT RESOURCE

This bonus item is the most important. I added it because I was watching a show on Food Network® with my wife and there was a story on Dave Thomas, the founder of Wendy's®.

Dave Thomas lived and breathed Wendy's® right up until the day he died. His family life suffered. But, his business was successful.

If you asked his kids, they'd tell you, "Dad was always gone." Is this the memory you want your kids to have?

When I was growing up, my dad worked wild "shifts." Sometimes he'd work days, then swing shift, then "graveyard" shift. I liked days the most since he was home in the afternoon so we could hang out with him and work around the house with him.

The other shifts stunk. He was gone when my brother

and I were home. Fortunately, he saw the writing on the wall early. He took courses and moved up in the company he worked for into a job that was better paying, and offered more family-friendly hours.

That change made a huge difference. Since you're most likely a dentist if you're reading this, you probably already have fairly family-friendly hours. Or, at least you should.

I thought success at an early age was about bank account size. I paid the price for it.

I know better now as I get to spend as much time as I want with my girls. All three. Well, four if you include the dog. My wife loves it, I love it and my girls get the benefit of "hangin'" with their dad. They are fun, smart and really help me keep things in perspective. I love it.

What I'm trying to tell you here is DO NOT ignore your family. They are great resources if you allow them to be. In the tough times, family unity is critical. It's what will make the best of times even better.

WRAP-UP

Did you notice how many of these items dealt with SPENDING MONEY vs. making it? You see, for most businesspeople, the challenge is saving money, not making it. Once you crack the "how to make it" code, the hard part begins. You know the saying, "A fool and his money are soon parted."

You have to protect your earnings, be attentive to them, and grow them. If you add to their flock, they will, in kind, give back in return. It's called compound interest, and you need to get some. Soon. Today. Now.

RESOURCES

Resources to check out for Jerry Jones Direct & other companies he likes:

www.JerryJonesDirect.com

www.ButtsInOps.com

www.ClearPathSociety.com

www.TrustETC.com - THE place for self-directed IRAs and 401(k)s

Made in the USA
San Bernardino, CA
04 February 2015